—— *Best of the* ——

WIDENER

Collection

LEXINGTON, KENTUCKY

ECLIPSE
PRESS

Best of the
WIDENER
Collection
Images from Racing's Golden Era

BLOOD-HORSE PUBLICATIONS

Library of Congress Control Number: 2008928613

ISBN 978-1-58150-194-0

Printed in China
First Edition: 2008

a division of
Blood-Horse Publications
PUBLISHERS SINCE 1916

CONTENTS

Foreword 6

Everyday Life 9

Horses 37

People 125

The Sporting Life 187

FOREWORD

The *Best of the Widener Collection* provides a fascinating glimpse of the horses, people, and racetrack life in and around New York from 1890 to 1910. From more than 1,000 images in the collection, Eclipse Press selected 150 that showcase the talents of John C. Hemment, one of the most respected photographers of the era.

Hemment was born in Cambridgeshire, England, and was educated in a country school before attending college in Peterborough for three years. Needing to earn his own living, he found employment in a retail draper's shop. He moved to London and secured a position in a clothing house, where he learned the art of cutting and designing children's clothing. In October 1879, he arrived in the United States and secured a position in a wholesale clothing house as a cutter. His love of athletics and outdoor sports led him to become interested in photography. Having competed in skating races around England, setting records for quarter- and half-mile distances, he was fascinated with finding a way to help judges determine the winner of a close race. Purchasing a camera and a tripod, he started photographing intercollegiate football, baseball, and track-and-field events. He was convinced that instantaneous photography could be used to capture the real winner in all close athletic contests

In 1890 Sheepshead Bay and Monmouth Park hired Hemment as the "official photographer" to take accurate pictures of the finishes of horse races. Sheepshead Bay provided a room, just above the judges' stand, for Hemment's camera and developing equipment. His photographs proved so valuable he became the official photographer for Coney Island, Brooklyn, and Saratoga racetracks. His experiments with dif-

Joseph E. Widener with jockey William Donahue

ferent cameras, lenses, shutter speeds, and developing techniques set a new standard for photographing horse races. Skillful at capturing the finish, he also took his camera to all other areas of the racetrack.

Each photograph tells its own story.

He took photos of such celebrated horses as Salvator, Tenny, Firenze, Henry of Navarre, Kingston, and Domino. The written word could now be illustrated with photographs to show people the real character of these horses. Paddock scenes of the Whitneys, the Vanderbilts, the Dwyer brothers, jockeys Isaac Murphy and Willie Simms, and trainers such as James G. Rowe Sr. and Frank McCabe depict both professional relationships and social gatherings. Trainers and jockeys discuss last-minute riding strategy. Owners chat with friends and inspect the competition. The stable area shows the everyday life of feeding, grooming, and caring for the horse as well as relaxation and leisure activities. Viewing these photographs takes one back to another era.

Hemment predicted that every racing association and athletic club in the country would require an official photographer. He also believed the great daily newspapers would employ expert instantaneous photographers. His predictions were right. Hemment's photographs appeared in *Illustrated Sporting News*, *Harper's Weekly*, *Collier's Weekly*, and *New York Journal*.

He did not devote all his time to photographing horse racing. In 1898 the U.S. government contracted him to photograph the wreckage of the *USS Maine* in Havana, Cuba. Securing several commissions from pictorial papers, Hemment packed up his photographic equipment and headed to Cuba. He documented the destruction of the *Maine*, camp life, and military operations. His experiences during the Spanish-American War are chronicled in his book *Cannon and Camera*.

We have noted owner, breeder, and patron of the Turf Joseph E. Widener to thank for this collection of Hemment's photos. Widener had in his possession seven albums of Hemment photographs. He gave the albums to Gayle Mohney, a prominent Lexington attorney. Mohney gave the albums to *The Blood-Horse*. Through the years *The Blood-Horse* has used the Hemment photos to illustrate numerous magazine articles and books. These photos clearly show Hemment's passion and attention to detail. Seen through Hemment's eyes, the racetrack comes alive, offering a glimpse at the pageantry and traditions of racing.

— CATHY SCHENCK
KEENELAND HEAD LIBRARIAN

EVERYDAY
Life

Bowlers and boaters: Racegoers at Sheepshead Bay note the scratches and additions to the day's race card. Built by a group of prominent New York City businessmen on the site of the Coney Island Jockey Club, Sheepshead Bay opened in 1884. Its premier event was the Suburban Handicap, today a fixture at Belmont Park. The track was shuttered during New York's ban on betting from late 1910 to 1913 and never reopened for racing.

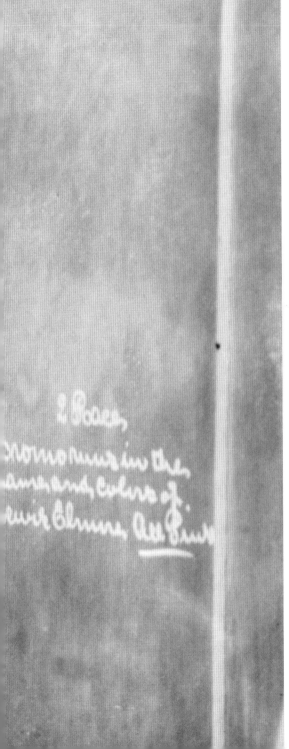

Bookmakers dictated the odds at racetracks well into the twentieth century. Pari-mutuel wagering gradually replaced bookmakers, with New York racing the major holdout until as late as 1940.

A family enters the main gate at the racecourse in Savannah, Georgia. The Civil War had decimated racing in the South, but the sport returned periodically to Savannah. In 1908, the Savannah Jockey Club opened a track at Thunderbolt, a suburb, for winter racing.

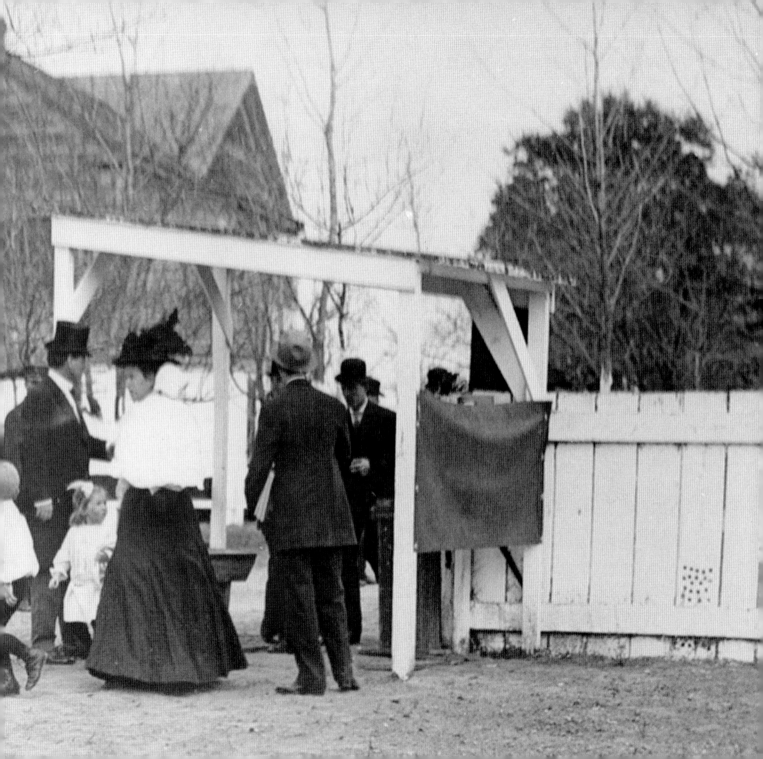

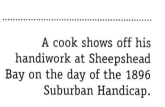

A cook shows off his handiwork at Sheepshead Bay on the day of the 1896 Suburban Handicap.

Stable boys while away the time shooting dice.

Race riding has always been a dangerous profession, but until the invention of the safety helmet in the mid-1950s, jockey deaths were comon. Until that time jockeys rode with a light skullcap covered by a silk cap. Left, trainer Thomas Hitchcock (in light suit) looks on at jockey James Rowan on a stretcher after being thrown. Above, jockey Fred Littlefield is helped off course after a fall.

Stable boys and their mascot: Child labor reached its peak in the early decades of the twentieth century and many youngsters worked at racetracks, essentially as indentured servants. Not until 1938 did the federal government impose minimum ages of employment and hours of work for children.

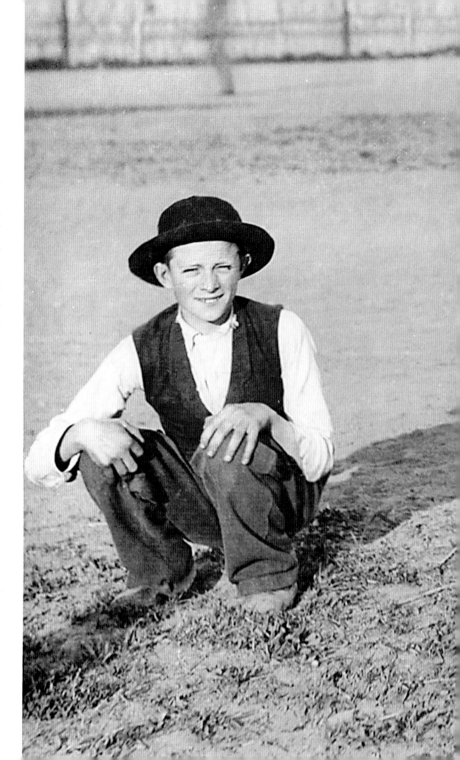

A horse looks out its stall during the winter meet at Guttenburg Race Track in northern New Jersey. The Guttenburg track, known for its gambling scandals, winter racing, and "horses who can't earn their oats at the bigger tracks," according to the *New York Times*, burned down in 1910, several years after racing had ceased there.

A string of horses heads to the track for morning exercise.

Grooms, also known as rubbers, return to the stables. African-Americans composed much of the labor force on the backsides of American racetracks in the late nineteenth century and early twentieth century.

Irish Lad gets rubbed down after a race. Owned by Harry Payne Whitney and Herman B. Duryea, Irish Lad won a thrilling 1903 Brooklyn Handicap before a crowd of nearly 30,000 fans, beating post-time favorite Gunfire, owned by Whitney's father, William C. Whitney.

Racehorses outfitted in coolers go for their evening walk.

....

Hell Gate Stable was the highly successful but short-lived racing operation of Frank Ehret, son of a New York brewery magnate. Ehret dispersed his stable of twenty-six horses, including the stakes-winning Yorkville Belle, at Tattersall's in 1892 for a total of $228,250. "A better sold lot of horses hardly ever passed under the hammer ... " the *New York Times* reported.

HORSES

Right, future Kentucky Derby winner Agile, on the inside, dead heats with Red Friar in the Youngsters Stake at Gravesend on June 15, 1904. Above, 1902 Kentucky Derby winner Alan-a-Dale is shown in a race warmup.

Blessed with matinee idol looks — a gleaming chestnut coat, four white stockings, a blaze, and a flaxen tail — California-bred Alsono caught the fancy of Mrs. H.P. Whitney and Mrs. H.B. Duryea, who purchased him at a Saratoga auction and raced him under their stable name, "Mr. Roslyn." Alsono won his very first start in the ladies' silks, green with white hoops, green sleeves, and green cap.

Left, four o' clock must have been the witching hour for August Belmont's Beldame, who was on her most unladylike behavior when going to the post before the Ladies Stakes on May 21, 1904. The champion filly, also pictured above, bolted and was pulled up by her substitute rider before bolting again and dumping the unwanted burden on her back. Maneuvering through the gap to the backstretch with the "agility of a polo pony," the fugitive ran all over the barn area before being caught by a stablehand and returned to the start. None the worse for wear, she won the Ladies Stakes in a canter.

Left, August Belmont with John Hyland (right), one of the filly's trainers, bred and raced Beldame but leased her to his business associate Newton Bennington, above. Right, born into a family that operated outlaw tracks in the Midwest, Frank O'Neill, Beldame's regular jockey, began riding races at age ten. He later moved to France and was leading jockey there.

Willie Simms dismounts Ben Brush after their win in the 1897 Suburban Handicap. Champion Ben Brush was sold to Mike Dwyer during the colt's two-year-old year. The 1896 Kentucky Derby winner was regularly ridden by Simms, the only African-American jockey to win the Kentucky Derby, the Preakness, and the Belmont. According to the *Spirit of the Times*, when Simms saw the deep cuts his spurs had inflicted in Ben Brush during the colt's hard-fought Derby win, he wept for shame.

Best Man, bred by Queen Victoria and winner of the July Cup at Newmarket Race Course in 1894. Note the use of the longer stirrups by the English jockeys. Willie Simms introduced the short-stirrup American style when he rode in England in 1895, but the style was looked upon with disdain until another American jockey, Tod Sloan, popularized it by winning races there.

Inset, James Ben Ali Haggin's Waterboy, the champion handicap horse in 1903, takes the sophomore star Broomstick to school in a Brighton Beach allowance race on July 20, 1904. Broomstick, owned by Captain S.S. Brown, used his third-place effort to catapult to an easy victory over Bobadil in the Travers Stakes at Saratoga on August 9.

Goughacres Stable's Bryn Mawr wins the 1904 Preakness Stakes over Wotan and the filly Dolly Spanker (on rail). Due to a change in the Maryland racing climate, perhaps caused in part by competition from Benning racetrack located near Washington, D.C., the Preakness was not held at Pimlico but in New York from 1890 to 1909. These are known as "the lost Preaknesses."

J.R. Keene owned and bred the handsome Colin, shown left with his handler. One of the greatest American racehorses, Colin retired undefeated in fifteen races, including the Belmont Stakes. Colin's prowess as a racehorse prompted his trainer, James G. Rowe Sr., to state he wanted as his epitaph "He trained Colin."

Above, shown as a broodmare, Correction, a full sister to the great Domino, was the best sprinting mare of her day. Right, for a horse born so crooked in his hind legs that none thought he would ever race, legendary Standardbred Dan Patch so dominated his sport that no opponent dared face him. Yet his popularity drew crowds of thousands just to see him race against the clock. World-renowned actress Lilly Langtree paid him a visit, a young Harry Truman wrote him a fan letter, and Dwight Eisenhower went to see him at the Kansas State Fair. Shown here in 1903 being driven by Myron McHenry, Dan Patch raced with a sulky specially designed to accommodate his crooked left hock. Dan Patch lost only two heats in his career and was never defeated in a race.

Above, this Pompeiian-styled clubhouse stood as a palatial hallmark of beautiful Morris Park on Long Island, the track often called the Newmarket of America and the site of the famous match race starring Domino, Clifford, and Henry of Navarre. Left, the crowd gathered in the grandstand and on the track apron for the famous race among the three rivals that dominated headlines in the racing world in 1894. More than 25,000 fans streamed through the gates to witness this red-letter event that would determine the most outstanding horse of the year.

Left, James R. and Foxhall Keene's Domino was undefeated as a juvenile and had only been beaten once when he faced Clifford and Henry of Navarre in the celebrated match race. Above, Foxhall Keene talks with his trainer Albert Cooper, second from left, the man responsible for giving Domino his early lessons. So surprised by Domino's brilliant speed the first time he tried the colt on the track, Cooper worked him again the next day with the same result.

Above, James R. Keene, shown with Domino grazing, benefited from his son's astute purchase of Domino when they merged stables in 1893. Far left, Billy Lakeland, Domino's trainer, made "the Black Whirlwind" one of the most popular horses in America in the mid-1890s. Left, Fred Taral, known for his exuberant use of the whip, rode Domino so vigorously that Domino recognized the jockey on sight. The horse would become so agitated he could be mounted only by being blindfolded.

Left, Kentucky horseman Byron Mc-Clelland purchased Henry of Navarre, opposite with Henry Griffin up, for $3,000 and developed the handsome chestnut into the leading horse in America in 1894. With a regal bearing worthy of his namesake, the French Huguenot king, Henry of Navarre had been a favorite of all who dealt with him, so beloved in fact that when as a yearling he was led to the auction ring to be sold, the farm staff wept.

Left, August Belmont (with umbrella) talks to his trainer, John Hyland, and an unidentified jockey. After much persuasion, Belmont purchased Henry of Navarre for $25,000 during the colt's four-year-old racing year and turned him over to trainer Hyland. Right, Alonzo "Lonnie" Clayton guided Henry of Navarre to the upset victory over Domino and Clifford in the great match race at Morris Park in 1894. In 1892 the fifteen-year-old Clayton rode Azra to win the Kentucky Derby, thereby becoming the youngest jockey ever to win the historic race.

Left, long considered one of the great jockeys in America, Willie Simms rode the consistent, stalwart Clifford, opposite, for the owner-trainer combination of John W. Rogers, above left, and Robert Rose, above right.

In a matched battle between the leading three-year-olds and the top older horse, the fan favorite Domino led Henry of Navarre and Clifford during the opening stages of the race, inset. Domino failed to carry his brilliant speed over the nine furlongs and fell behind. A determined Henry of Navarre held off a steely challenge from the older Clifford to earn accolades as the leading horse in America in 1894.

Hamburg, owned and trained by John E. Madden, inset left, performed brilliantly at two but not without a tussle. Madden called Hamburg the toughest horse he ever trained, but once tamed the son of Hanover was quick to exercise and eager to eat. Burdened with the highest weights ever carried by a juvenile, Hamburg won stakes races carrying up to 135 pounds. Having been sold as a three-year-old to copper king Marcus Daly for $40,000 and one silver dollar, the colt continued to perform well. His one hundred-length victory in the Brighton Cup prompted world-famous jockey Tod Sloan to call him "the only great horse I ever rode."

Hamburg's daughter Hamburg Belle, the
leading two-year-old filly in 1903, defeated
a stellar field in the rich Futurity Stakes.
Hamburg Belle was owned by Sydney Paget
and trained by A.J. Joyner.

August Belmont's Hastings, outside, accelerates in the stretch
to catch Handspring and win the
Belmont Stakes at Morris Park,
thereby turning the tables on
an earlier loss to his nemesis.
Belmont purchased Hastings
for a record price of $37,000.
An ill-tempered horse who
had inherited the disposition
of his dam, Hastings resented
training and exhibited extreme
displeasure at being saddled. The
exercise lads and jockeys were
hard-pressed to control him. His
transition to the pastoral life of
a stallion did nothing to change
his disposition, and the grooms
armed themselves with clubs to
keep him in line. Leading sire in
1902, Hastings sired Fair Play,
who sired Man o' War.

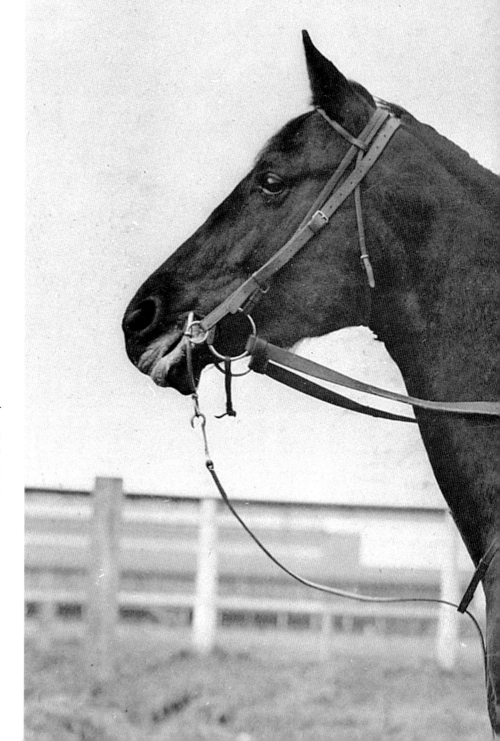

Hello, ridden by Frank O'Neill, bears a stately countenance during his training regimen.

Left, rank outsider Howard Mann returns to be unsaddled after an upset win in the 1897 Brooklyn Handicap. Substituting from the bench when the pacesetter for his more illustrious stablemate had to be scratched, Howard Mann benefited from a cleverly orchestrated ride by his jockey Skeets Martin. The victory brought about a betting coup for his owner, the inveterate gambler G.E. "Pittsburgh Phil" Smith, who is thought to have pocketed at least $75,000 off the bookmakers. Above, sprint specialist Irene Lindsay was a bit of a hard-luck horse, barely missing some important stakes wins.

Although cursed with an intractable nature that often compromised his racing success, Lamplighter, above and left, with Willie Simms wearing the Rancocas Stable's silks, was the leading older horse in 1893 in spite of his defeat by Marcus Daly's Tammany in a much-heralded match race.

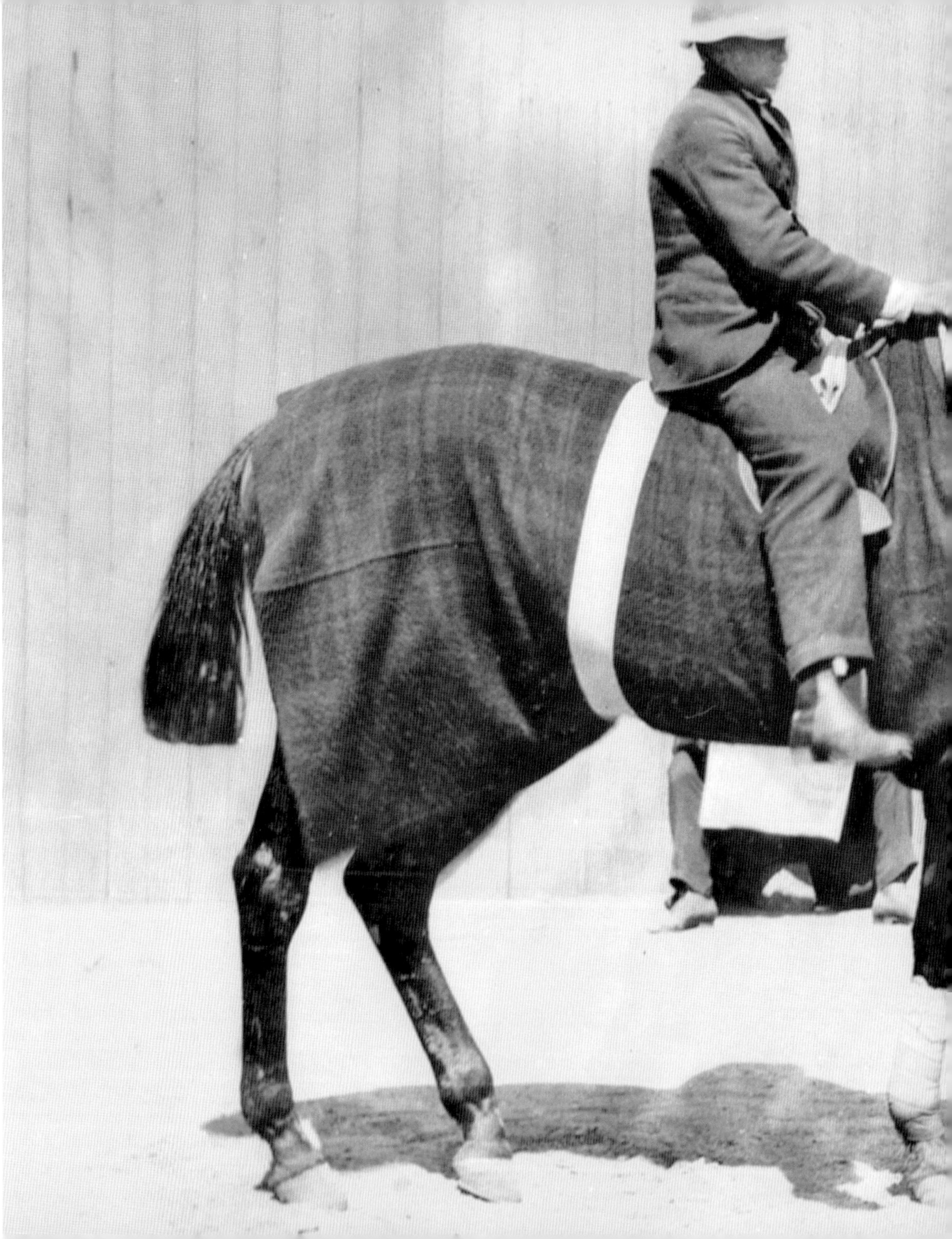

Mike Dwyer's Longstreet, known for his sulky disposition, won an 1891 match race against the well-regarded Tenny and validated his owner's belief in his talents.

Left, perhaps the original "Big Mac," McChesney, the star of the West, was trained by Sam Hildreth, right. Of all the great horses that Hildreth owned or trained, McChesney was his favorite. James Ben Ali Haggin bought McChesney for a stallion prospect but sold him to a buyer in Argentina, where the flashy chestnut became a great progenitor of polo ponies.

One of the most popular horses of the era, McChesney, shown above warming up for his Twin Cities engagement, attracted quite a following in the paddock after his win in the handicap, right. McChesney's stable companion was a parrot named Dick who possessed rather salty language. "McChesney, McChesney, oh, McChesney," the first cries heard in the stable in the morning came from Dick, who slept on a beam above McChesney's stall. The parrot would spend hours perched on McChesney's back and the horse seemed to welcome the company.

Above, an icon of harness racing, the undefeated Nancy Hanks was named for Abraham Lincoln's mother. Although small in size, the bay filly was large in talent and set a world record, trotting a mile in 2:04 and lowering the previous record by more than four seconds. Her no-nonsense discipline masked a temperament that was anything but docile. Right, Meddler was imported to this country when his owner George Baird, a fiery-tempered Scot, died prematurely, nullifying all the colt's stakes engagements according to the rules of racing at the time. American breeder W.H. Forbes purchased the undefeated Meddler as a stallion prospect. Forbes' death sent Meddler to the formidable stud barn of W.C. Whitney. Meddler led the American sire list in 1906.

Above, James R. Keene's juvenile star Peter Pan posts an impressive victory in the 1906 Surf Stakes at Sheepshead Bay, a performance that prompted the chart writer to brand him "a coming crackerjack." Right, Peter Pan, number 3, is shown with apprentice jockey Herman Radtke wearing the famous blue polka-dotted silks of Keene's Castleton Farm. Radtke had earlier in the year set a world's record for the number of winning mounts (twenty-one) in a week. In 1907 Peter Pan won the Belmont Stakes and eventually became a leading sire for H.P. Whitney, who purchased the son of Commando for $38,000 from the Keene estate's dispersal sale.

Proper, a handsome Thoroughbred type, ridden by jockey Eugene Hildebrand, sports a saddle with lead weights to add impost for racing in handicaps.

Captain S.S. Brown's and John W. Rogers' Pickpocket, with jockey Tony Hamilton up, was a horse gifted with brilliant speed and cursed with a terrific temper that earned him the reputation of being one of the Turf's biggest rogues. Note the blinkers, or hood as it was known in its day, designated as the "badge of a rogue." Pickpocket's performance in any race was dictated by the kindliness with which he ran. He clearly loved a heavy track and didn't mind a fast one.

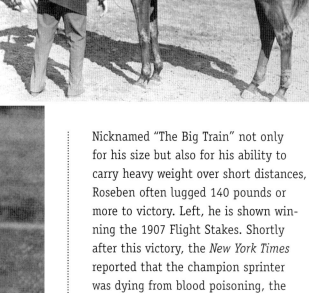

Nicknamed "The Big Train" not only for his size but also for his ability to carry heavy weight over short distances, Roseben often lugged 140 pounds or more to victory. Left, he is shown winning the 1907 Flight Stakes. Shortly after this victory, the *New York Times* reported that the champion sprinter was dying from blood poisoning, the result of an injury sustained when he stepped on a sharp stone. Roseben survived and raced two more years.

Rock Sand was imported for stallion duty by August Belmont, but the arrival of the $125,000 purchase was not without incident. It seemed the English Triple Crown winner would not walk the plank. For more than an hour after the *Minneapolis* had docked at Pier 15 on New York's North River, Rock Sand's handlers, and even Belmont himself, could not persuade him to forsake the relative saftey of the ship and walk down the narrow gangplank to the pier. No amount of pushing, pulling, wheedling, or cajoling worked on the apprehensive stallion. He so rejected the idea of departing over that narrow piece of wood that he lay down in the cramped quarters of the steamer deck, stressing his handlers who feared he might injure himself. To the rescue came John O'Keefe of the traffic squad, who rode his mount up the gangplank while an interested Rock Sand watched. That was all the English import needed as he willingly followed O'Keefe's horse back down the gangplank and into the waiting transport that would ferry him to the train station for his transfer to Belmont's Kentucky farm.

Rock Sand became the broodmare sire of Man o' War.

James Ben Ali Haggin loved Salvator, shown above with his trainer Matt Byrnes, so much that ten years after buying him as a yearling for $4,500, he purchased the Kentucky farm, Elmendorf, where the colt had been foaled. And what was there not to love? A dark chestnut sporting a blaze and four white stockings, Salvator was faultlessly made with a magnificent shoulder, a short back, and powerful hindquarters. His good looks made the colt a fan favorite at two and three. At four, he became a hero and his match race with Tenny a red-letter event. As handsome as Salvator was, Tenny, left, was not. He never outgrew the awkward stage of youth, and although he remained an undersized, swayback horse, he could run. The match race was a much-anticipated event, and the outcome matched the expectations. The two hit the wire so close together only the judges' decision could separate them and declare Salvator the victor.

Inset, third time was a charm for Oneck Stable's Sir Walter, shown with the hot-tempered Sam Doggett in the irons. In 1894 Doggett nearly had his license revoked for striking another jockey across the face with a whip and attempting to force horse and rider over the rail. After finishing second in two previous runnings of the Brooklyn Handicap, Sir Walter won the 1896 running over the famed Clifford. Left, Strathmeath, owned and trained by the shrewd Green B. Morris, bore his owner's silks to victory in the Junior Champion Stakes on the same card as the Salvator-Tenny match race.

No more stout-hearted juvenile colt could be found on the American racing scene in 1909 than James R. Keene's Sweep (shown with jockey James Butwell up), who carried 126 pounds to win the rich Futurity and give Keene his fifth victory and his third successive homebred winner (following Colin in 1907 and Maskette in 1908) of the country's most important juvenile race. Trained by James G. Rowe Sr., Sweep would go on to win the 1910 Belmont Stakes at three. Retired to his owner's Castleton Stud, Sweep led the general sire list twice. He is the broodmare sire of two Triple Crown winners: War Admiral and Whirlaway.

Inset, James R. Keene had little use for a small, lop-eared foal born at his Castleton Farm in 1902. But there was a certain something about the bay colt that was most appealing to the owner's son, Foxhall, who changed his father's mind and who named the ugly duckling Sysonby for a favorite hunting lodge in England. And trainer James G. Rowe Sr. resorted to a bit of skullduggery by faking an illness for the colt to keep Sysonby from being shipped to England. Sysonby might have been plain, but when he launched himself in flight, the beauty of his stride was what people noticed. Above, on his way to becoming one of the era's greatest horses, Sysonby showed the field his heels in the 1904 Saratoga Special.

But for a groom, a bribe, and W.C. Whitney's speedy filly Artful, above, Sysonby might have gone through his racing career unbeaten. Sixteen horses faced the starter in the 1904 Futurity, the richest race of the American Turf, with three undefeated juveniles, Sysonby among them, garnering most of the attention. At the finish, however, the maiden filly Artful waylaid the field by five widening lengths in track-record time. Uncharacteristically, Sysonby never unleashed his powerful stride, shown left in a workout, and finished third. One of the Keene grooms, later caught sporting a large roll of bills, confessed to tranquilizing Sysonby prior to the race. Sysonby never again tasted defeat. Sysonby, above left with jockey Arthur Redfern, died in his stall at Sheepshead Bay in 1906. More than 5,000 attended his burial.

Left, W.C. Whitney dominated racing at the turn of the twentieth century. One of his runners, Tanya, shown above, set the world's record for four and a half furlongs. In 1905 Tanya became the second filly to win the Belmont Stakes, emulating Ruthless' 1867 inaugural victory. Much to the chagrin of grizzled old-timers of the Turf, the turn of the century found more fashionable women, especially wives of prominent owners such as Mrs. H.P. Whitney, right, visiting the paddock to see their horses. According to the *New York Times*, "Many a fair visitor went about unescorted and paid no heed to the numerous photographers taking snap shots at every interesting group."

A custom of the times, the warmup gallops were mere canters over the track and offered no clues into the race for those seeking insight that would serve them well in the betting rings. Left, the lovely mare who won the 1906 Brooklyn Handicap, Tokalon, and whose name taken from Greek means "the beautiful thing," warms up for a race. Above, unlike today, starters were not accompanied to the post by a lead pony. The top stakes horse Africander, who set a world record in the 1904 Lawrence Realization Stakes, walks calmly to the post.

A postrace photo of Terrifier, a handicap horse
of the 1890s

Sydney Paget's filly Tradition won Saratoga's Alabama Stakes, a prestigious and historic race even in 1905. She also won the Gazelle and Neptune stakes racing for Paget, who at one time partnered with W.C. Whitney in the Whitney racing enterprises.

Above, Francis R. Hitchcock's Vendor was among the leading two-year-olds of 1905. His victory in the Waldorf Stakes, a companion event to the Astoria Stakes, carried with the winning purse and trophy a dinner hosted at the Waldorf Astoria Hotel by the winning owner to celebrate his good fortune. These dinner stakes were originally designed as friendly matches among owners vying for the honor of hosting the dinner party. Right, although plagued with unsoundness as a result of inheriting the bad feet of his sire, Star Shoot, Uncle won seven races from twelve starts and got within a length of defeating Colin in the 1907 Saratoga Special. Uncle sired 1914 Kentucky Derby winner Old Rosebud and was the broodmare sire of 1927 Kentucky Derby winner Clyde Van Dusen.

Shown in a prerace warmup, Whimsical in 1906
became the second filly to win the Preakness Stakes.

PEOPLE
Owners

John Madden, left, the son of Irish immigrants, became one of the most successful breeders, owners, and trainers of the first quarter of the twentieth century. A physically imposing individual, Madden excelled early as an athlete, becoming an amateur boxing champion and skilled trotting-horse driver. The wheeler-dealer Madden was an adept horse trader through whose hands many a great horse passed. "Better to sell and repent than keep and repent" is one of the maxims often attributed to him. His sale of the top racehorse Hamburg enabled him to buy a farm in Kentucky that he named Hamburg Place, birthplace of five Kentucky Derby winners.

Right, Foxhall Keene, with walking stick, and trainer James G. Rowe Sr. Keene, the son of powerful owner James R. Keene, wrote in his memoirs, "When Rowe took our horses in charge, things began to change … Even old Voter came to life, and his recovery was a nice piece of veterinary work on Rowe's part." Above, the Keene stable parades on the grounds at Saratoga in 1903.

Pierre Lorillard, far left, built up a large fortune in the tobacco business and established Rancocas Stable, the era's premier stable. He raced several successful Thoroughbreds in the United States and in Europe, achieving international fame with the American colt Iroquois, who in 1881 won the English Derby, St. Leger Stakes, and Prince of Wales's Stakes. Lorillard's success in Europe led to a partnership with Lord William Beresford, who, impressed with American methods, began using American jockey Tod Sloan. Sloan's monkey crouch in the saddle led other riders worldwide to emulate his style. Right, John Sanford inherited Hurricana Farm when his father, Stephen, died in 1913. A major figure in racing and U.S. representative from New York, Sanford raced a number of top horses and in 1916 won the Kentucky Derby with his colt George Smith. In 1923 Sanford became the first American to win the English Grand National, the most prestigious steeplechase race in the world, with his horse Sergeant Murphy. In 1933 Sanford won the American Grand National with Best Play. Sanford was a member of the New York Racing Commission. The Sanford Stakes, run annually at Saratoga Race Course, is named in his family's honor.

Kentucky-born James Ben Ali Haggin, second from left, struck it rich during the California gold rush. At the turn of the century, he owned more horses than anyone else in the nation and at one point owned 10,000 acres in the Bluegrass, including Elmendorf Farm and the famed Green Hills mansion. Above, Thomas Hitchcock was regarded as the greatest steeple-chase trainer in the history of the Turf and twice won the Grand National Steeplechase. As a young man, Hitchcock captained the first American international polo team and is credited with popularizing the game in the 1920s. He also was the oldest commissioned officer to fly during World War I at age fifty-seven. Ironically, his son Tommy was the youngest commissioned officer, at the age of seventeen, to fly in World War I. Hitchcock died at age eighty and Tommy, also an accomplished polo player, followed him three years later when his plane was shot down during World War II. He was forty-four.

Financier W.C. Whitney, far left, patriarch of the Whitney family and secretary of the Navy under President Cleveland, and August Belmont, a fellow New York banking magnate after whom the Belmont Stakes is named, ruled New York racing during their era. Right, H.P. Whitney (in light suit), was an avid sportsman, playing ten-goal polo and captaining his yacht in the America's Cup. At his Whitney Farm in Lexington, Whitney developed the American polo pony and also sent forth a phalanx of classic winners, including the 1915 Kentucky Derby winner Regret.

Above, H.P. Whitney and his wife, Gertrude, watch one of his runners being saddled. Right, H.B. Duryea, with walking stick, began buying and breeding horses around the turn of the century. A perennial sportsman, he was also a prominent yachtsman and breeder of dogs and gamecocks. In addition to a large estate in Old Westbury on Long Island, which was eventually sold to Henry Phipps as a wedding gift for his daughter, he owned a large "plantation" in Tennessee, where he conducted his breeding operations. Duryea was an associate of William C. Whitney, who for a long time raced his horses under Duryea's colors. Duryea was half owner with Harry Payne Whitney in Irish Lad, who won the Brooklyn Handicap in 1903 and the Metropolitan Handicap a year later. In 1910, Duryea moved his stable to Europe in response to antigambling legislation in New York and other states.

Above, Mrs. John Sanford (second from left) and Mrs. Tom Hitchcock (far right) at the races in Saratoga; right, Alfred Vanderbilt, holding walking stick, with a friend in the paddock, was a prominent owner and breeder fated to be remembered for his untimely death aboard the RMS *Lusitania*.

An afternoon at the races was considered a socially acceptable pastime for the privileged classes. Right, Henry J. Morris and Joseph E. Widener, a major figure in U.S. racing as majority owner of Belmont Park and founder of Hialeah Park in south Florida, talk in the paddock. An avid art collector, Widener was one of the founders of the National Gallery of Art in Washington, D.C.

PEOPLE
Trainers

Byron McClelland, seated center with his stable's employees, grew up in Lexington, Kentucky, and made his fame and fortune as a trainer. In his 1897 obituary he was proclaimed a "son of the sod" who was very well thought of by his fellow Turfmen. Nearly 3,000 attended his funeral after his death following "a malarial chill." McClelland started out as a jockey before his weight forced him to move on to training. His first training job of note was for Pennsylvania millionaire W.L. Scott, a heavy gambler for whom McClelland also placed bets. This venture was profitable the first two years, but the stable's fortunes turned the third year, and Scott quarreled with the trainer and refused to pay the "markers" McClelland had bet for him in his own name. The trainer went heavily into debt but managed to scrape together $120 to buy a yearling he later named Badge. The little guy became a grand weight carrier who won thousands of dollars. McClelland used his earnings to pay off every dollar of Scott's indebtedness with which he had been saddled. The later part of his career is much more well known. He owned Sally McClelland, Henry of Navarre, Halma, Caesarian, Prince Lief, Maceo, and several other lesser-known racehorses.

Left, Frank McCabe was a distinguished trainer of the late nineteenth century and early twentieth century. He trained Hall of Famer Hanover, as well as three consecutive Belmont winners: Inspector B., 1886; Hanover, 1887; Sir Dixon, 1888. During that same period, McCabe trained Tremont, who was unbeaten in thirteen starts as a two-year-old in 1886. McCabe's other Hall of Fame horses were Kingston, who won 89 of 138 starts, including 30 stakes, and retired as America's leading money winner at $140,195; and Miss Woodford, the first horse bred and raced in America to earn more than $100,000. McCabe was inducted into the Hall of Fame in 2007.

Right, William Garth, a popular trainer of the first quarter of the twentieth century, trained 1920 Kentucky Derby winner Paul Jones and finished second in 1923 with Martingale. As a young man he was the greatest wrestler of his day in the East and a skillful equestrian.

Plucked as a youngster from his job at a newsstand, James G. Rowe Sr. became a successful teenage jockey before developing into a training legend. He also served for a time as a starter. In fifty years, Rowe conditioned thirty-two champions for five owners. His notable horses included multiple champions Miss Woodford, Commando, Sysonby, the undefeated Colin, and the Kentucky Derby-winning filly Regret. "Rowe was a rough taskmaster," fellow trainer Mose Goldbatt said after Rowe's death. "He neither spared himself nor his helpers. Up before light every day of the year, no matter what the weather might be, he always had his help up and doing. When an ailing horse required his attention, he would stay with it indefinitely."

Right, trainer Green B. Morris, on horseback, achieved a remarkable triumph in 1882 when he won the Kentucky Derby with 30-1 shot Apollo. That year the Dwyer brothers owned a colt named Runnymede who was the even-money favorite by virtue of his record and the skill of his jockey, Jimmy McLaughlin. But in a sensational finish Apollo won by a half-length to Runnymede, and Mike Dwyer lost a small fortune. Though Morris would never repeat the Derby win, he had a successful training career with horses such as Sir Dixon, Strathmeath, and Freeman, among many others. Left, on the rail, trainer William P. Burch and owner Francis Hitchcock observe the activities on the track. Burch served in the Confederate Army and in the aftermath of the war's destruction set out to earn a living racing horses. A member of the Hall of Fame and the patriarch of a training dynasty, he was the father of conditioner Preston Burch and grandfather of Elliot Burch.

Above, trainers Enoch Wishard, left, and Andrew Jackson Joyner, center, share a track bench. Wishard ranked as the leading trainer in England in 1899, saddling fifty-four winners. Described as a genius by one British contemporary, Wishard allegedly admitted he was not averse to doping his horses but had found nothing that really worked. Joyner occupied a unique niche as a top-notch trainer for thirty years, working in the United States and England for prominent owners such as H.P. Whitney, August Belmont, and George D. Widener. He trained outstanding horses such as Fair Play, Whisk Broom II, and Eight-Thirty, handling also the greatest number of horses for a trainer of his time. "Under the arrangement Trainer Joyner has made with his employers, he simply trains whatever they send him," wrote the *New York Times* in 1905, "and, though seemingly impossible tasks have been set for him on occasions, he has showed most satisfactory results." Right, Green Morris and a fellow trainer look over a condition book.

PEOPLE

Jockeys

One of the greatest jockeys in American racing history, Isaac Murphy, left, was the first jockey to win three Kentucky Derbys, and his win rate of 44 percent remains unequaled. Known as the "Colored Archer," a reference to Fred Archer, a prominent English jockey of the time, Murphy was a master of pace and often won races by narrow margins as when he urged Tulla Blackburn, shown above on the outside, to pass Strideaway for a narrow victory in a sweepstakes at Coney Island on July 1, 1891. Murphy died at age thirty-five in Lexington, Kentucky, and over time his unmarked grave was forgotten. Murphy's grave eventually was rediscovered, and his remains were buried next to Man o' War's at the Kentucky Horse Park. Murphy was the first jockey to be inducted into the National Museum of Racing and Hall of Fame.

Left, black jockeys dominated American racing in the late nineteenth century until prize money increased and riders began earning a percentage of the winning purse. Above, George Taylor was one of the best-known jockeys in the 1880s and early '90s. Originally from England, he rode in the United States for twelve years until he was gravely injured during a race in 1893. Riding in a crowded field of fourteen on the narrow Gravesend track, Taylor got his leg pinned between his horse and the rail midway through the race, breaking bones in three places between his knee and ankle. In severe pain, Taylor was unable to control his horse, which took off and then fell. Taylor was thrown to the ground and was either stepped on or rolled over by the horse, further injuring his leg, which had to be amputated, ending his career.

Left, Anthony Hamilton won great fame and fortune riding for James Ben Ali Haggin, August Belmont, and other great men of the Turf. His 1891 wedding to Annie Messley drew attention in the *New York Times*. "The bride's family is a wealthy one. The groom is one of the most successful jockeys in America, and last season was chief jockey for the Belmont Stables," read the wedding announcement. "The bride is very light in complexion. Numerous wedding presents were received by the young people from their friends, both white and colored, among the collection being a handsome fruit stand from the colored jockey Isaac Murphy and his wife." Above, Willie Simms was the first jockey to use the short stirrup that gave the rider a crouching posture. En route to winning the U.S. riding title in 1894, Simms won back-to-back Belmont Stakes. The following year he raced in England where he became the first American jockey to win with an American horse in that country. There, he was ridiculed for his riding style, which was later popularized by Tod Sloan. Back home, Simms won the Kentucky Derby in 1896 on Ben Brush and again in 1898 aboard Plaudit. He is the only African-American jockey to win all of the classics.

Left to right, Sam Doggett, Willie Simms, and Fred Taral were among the most sought-after riders of their day. Doggett's temper, however, often found him afoul of the stewards while Taral's aggressiveness made some horses fear him.

Above Fred Taral, left, with fellow jockey Tod Sloan, unfortunately made his mark as a jockey with his more-than-liberal use of the whip. He rode the great racehorse Domino, who became so afraid of the rider he would quiver when Taral approached. A blanket had to be put over the colt's head so that Taral could mount him. When Taral had difficulty making weight in the United States, he rode and trained in Europe for a few years before the start of World War I. Right, Taral is shown aboard Marcus Daly's star Tammany, who won the Lawrence Realization, Withers, and Jerome stakes in 1892.

Left, Silas Veitch was a jockey-turned-horse trainer from Ontario, Canada, who raced horses in Saratoga Springs as early as the 1890s. Veitch had five children: Sidney, Sylvester, Thomas, Leo, and Ethel. All, except for Ethel, made their careers in the horse racing business as jockeys and trainers. His grandson John Veitch is well known in today's Thoroughbred racing world as a Hall of Fame trainer and racing steward. Right, Tod Sloan (with Jesse Lewishohn) popularized the forward seat style of riding, known as the monkey crouch, which eventually revolutionized the sport. During his short but spectacular career, Sloan enjoyed celebrity and the company of beautiful women, traveling with a valet and a lavish wardrobe. He inspired the character Yankee Doodle in the Broadway musical *Little Johnny Jones* and the Ernest Hemingway short story, "My Old Man."

Left, little is known today about jockeys Sweet and Gilbert. Right, Joe Notter, shown aboard Peter Pan, began his career as a ten-year-old stable boy before becoming a successful jockey. He won his first race at age thirteen on a 100-1 shot named Hydrangea. He is much more well known for piloting Regret, the first filly to win the Kentucky Derby. He also was the first to win the Handicap Triple Crown: the Metropolitan, Suburban, and Brooklyn handicaps of 1913, aboard Whisk Broom II. By age eighteen, Notter had gained too much weight to ride regularly. By reducing strenuously, he still received impressive mounts for significant stakes races, but he never rode more than twenty-one races per year in the last decade of his career.

Left, jockey James Frank Pohanka. Above, Walter Miller, shown returning to the winner's circle aboard Superman while the track is being harrowed before the next race, grew up in an Orthodox Jewish family but became fascinated with the racetrack as a youngster. His father, seeing the boy was smitten, consented to his son becoming a jockey. His first manager was his mother, though he later fell under the tutelage of "Sunny Jim" Fitzsimmons. He began riding professionally at age fourteen and went on to become one of the greatest jockeys of the early twentieth century. At age sixteen he rode a record 388 winners, including the Preakness winner that year, Whimsical. His record stood until Willie Shoemaker broke it in 1952. Later, when he could not make weight, he rode in Europe with considerable success. He was inducted into the National Thoroughbred Racing Hall of Fame in 1955.

Jockey Kelleher tumbled from E.H. Carle's Rufus during a 2½ mile steeplechase at Belmont Park on October 5, 1908. The chart states, "Rufus ran forwardly for 2 miles before coming to grief." Neither horse nor rider was seriously injured as both raced later in the year.

Left, James (Jim) McLaughlin, orphaned and homeless in his early teens, was taken in by trainer William Daly who taught him how to ride. He first competed in the Kentucky Derby in 1880, for the Dwyer Brothers Stable with trainer James G. Rowe Sr. The following year the team won the race on the future Hall of Fame horse Hindoo. He set the record for most wins by a jockey in the Belmont Stakes, six, when he rode Sir Dixon to a twelve-length victory in 1888. McLaughlin's record was matched by Eddie Arcaro in 1955. McLaughlin was the nation's leading jockey four consecutive times, from 1884 through 1887. He rode his last race in 1892, after which he worked as a trainer and racetrack official.

Right, Willie Knapp's relatively long career spanned the early decades of the 1900s. He is best known for riding Exterminator to victory in the 1918 Kentucky Derby when his regular mount, Sun Briar, the shining star of Willis Sharpe Kilmer's stable, trained poorly. Exterminator won by a length but still didn't win the respect of his owner, who referred to the angular-looking horse as a "billy goat." Knapp, meanwhile, went on the following year to ride H.P. Whitney's Upset to victory in the Sanford Memorial Stakes over the legendary Man o' War, who stable employees claim had nightmares for weeks after that lone defeat of his career. Knapp later became a trainer.

PEOPLE
Racetrack Characters

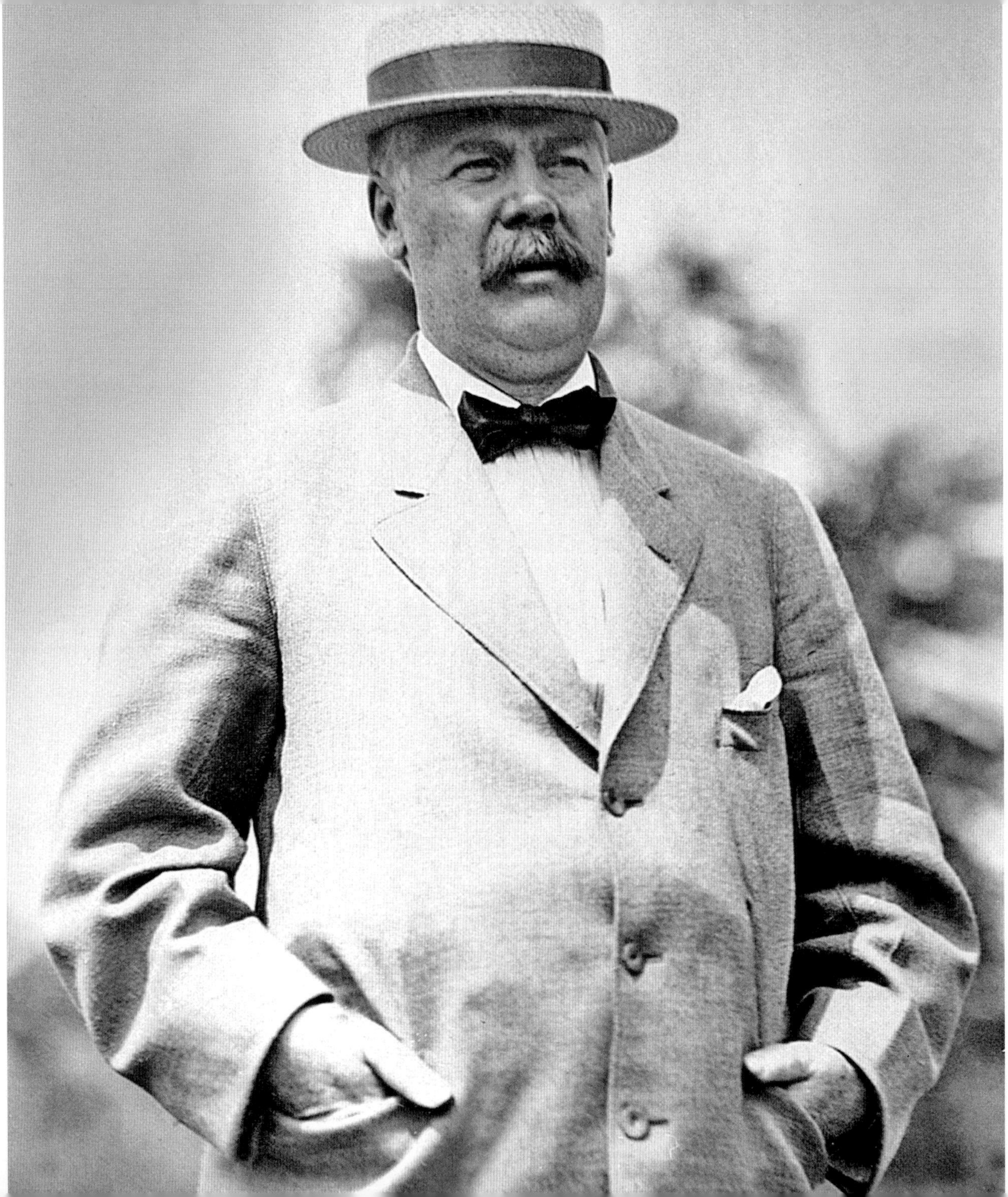

Left, Louisville tailor-turned-racetrack impressario Matt Winn helped make the Kentucky Derby the "most exciting two minutes in sports." The pudgy, cigar-smoking charmer wooed prominent East Coast columnists and wealthy horse owners in his off-season base at the Waldorf-Astoria towers in New York City. Right, John Warner "Bet-a-Million" Gates, right foreground, was an oil-and-steel tycoon and flamboyant gambler of the early 1900s who disdained vests in the summer to show off the three diamonds sparkling from his shirt. Gates would forego sleep to wager immense amounts in marathon two-to-three-day gambling sessions. The higher the stakes, the greater the thrill for Gates. Once when asked to limit his bets to $10,000 by Jockey Club chairman August Belmont II, who feared his exorbitant wagering would rile anti-gambling activists, Gates refused.

Left center, actress Lillian Russell enjoyed a day at the races and was a familiar figure at Saratoga. Famous for her beauty, voice, and acting talents, Russell also created a stir with her four marriages and friendship with gambler Diamond Jim Brady.

Right, Mars Cassidy started 50,000 racehorses in his lifetime. He is said to have sent horses away at practically every track open in the United States, Mexico, and Canada during his tenure. Always seeking to improve racing, he invented the first starting barrier, originally using a rubber device that stretched across the track and snapped at the signal. This was later replaced by webbing, and Cassidy was responsible for perfecting its mechanical parts.

Left in light hat, Pittsburgh Phil started out life as George E. Smith in Pennsylvania but showed himself as a more-than-able bettor, earning the nickname "Pittsburgh Phil" to distinguish himself from the brethren of other Smiths. He was so adept at picking horses that he gave up his job cutting cork. He moved to New York in 1887 "in search of a larger field," according to the *New York Times*, and became the leading bettor at tracks around the state. "He persistently ignored favorites and sought long prices against horses that in his judgment 'figured' to have the chance to win." He was so successful that he was asked, unofficially, to moderate his betting. His eventual ownership of a stable made The Jockey Club nervous, and stewards were ordered to reject his entries on the grounds that "the running of horses by so conspicuous a 'plunger' was detrimental to the turf." No wrongdoing was ever charged against him, and his racing privileges were later restored.

Right, Charles "Fatty" Bates was a well-known trainer, breeder, and driver in New York City, where he owned two stables with 100 horses on hand, in addition to a farm in Hubbard, Ohio, where he had at least another 150 horses. During the city's annual Horse Show week he would drive around a coach pulled by four horses, with "a boy in odd costume on a cock horse trailing behind," according to his obituary in the *New York Times*. Bates made a very good living selling "many a fine prize animal at a fancy price." He introduced docking trotters' tails and training them to high knee and hock action. He also held the world's record for making quick changes of horses to a road coach, his time being forty-two seconds, five seconds faster than his closest competitor.

Left, Walter Spencer Vosburgh started his lengthy and productive Turf career as a journalist for *Spirit of the Times*, the leading sports periodical of the 1880s and '90s, writing under the nom de plume "Vigilant." His most recognized writing effort was *American Racing, 1866-1921*, a work he undertook at The Jockey's Club's urging to preserve his racing recollections. When The Jockey Club was formed in 1894, Vosburgh served as its secretary, forfeit clerk, and handicapper. When the duties were later divided, he remained the official handicapper, keeping exhaustive records and staying up until two or three in the morning to study a handicap despite being an early riser. In 1933 Vosburg initiated the very first Experimental Free Handicap, which to this day still annually rates two-year-olds with regard to their expected performance as three-year-olds.

Right, the Prince of Wales, who was to become King George V in 1910, attends the races.

the
SPORTING
Life

Colonel William Jay and his wife coach in Central Park in 1896. Jay, the only son of John Jay, a former minister to Austria and a direct descendant of John Jay of Revolutionary War fame, was part of a family identified with the life and affairs of New York. The state's history is linked with the names of the Jays, the Astors, the Schuylers, and the Rensselaers. Embracing his father's antislavery views, he fought in the Civil War after graduating from Columbia. He served throughout the conflict, earning the rank of lieutenant colonel. He reentered Columbia to get his law degree when he returned and built up an extensive practice. In addition, he was one of the foremost horsemen in the country, starting the New York Coaching Club, one of the greatest influences on four-in-hand driving.

A tandem parade in Central Park, 1896: Prominent New Yorkers enjoyed showing off their fine harness horses in pairs and tandems, and Central Park was a favorite venue.

Gentleman attired for coaching: "To a remarakble degree the handling of good, spirited fours requires firmness and steadiness of hand, quickness of thought, rapid decision and unlimited nerve," the *New York Times* reported. Getting a four-in-hand in presentable condition also required a large investment, with a good coach costing upwards of $3,000; a good horse, $1,500; and driving aprons, $125 each.

New Yorkers show off their fine harness horses on the Harlem River Speedway. Amateur and professional drivers engaged in impromptu races, or "brushes," and these contests often drew thousands of spectators. The *New York Times* described the Speedway as the "world's greatest public speeding ground."

Polo at Prospect Park in Brooklyn could attract up to 20,000 spectators. Left, and above, far right, J.E. Cowdin, a nine-handicap player and a founder of the United States Polo Association, takes part in a match.

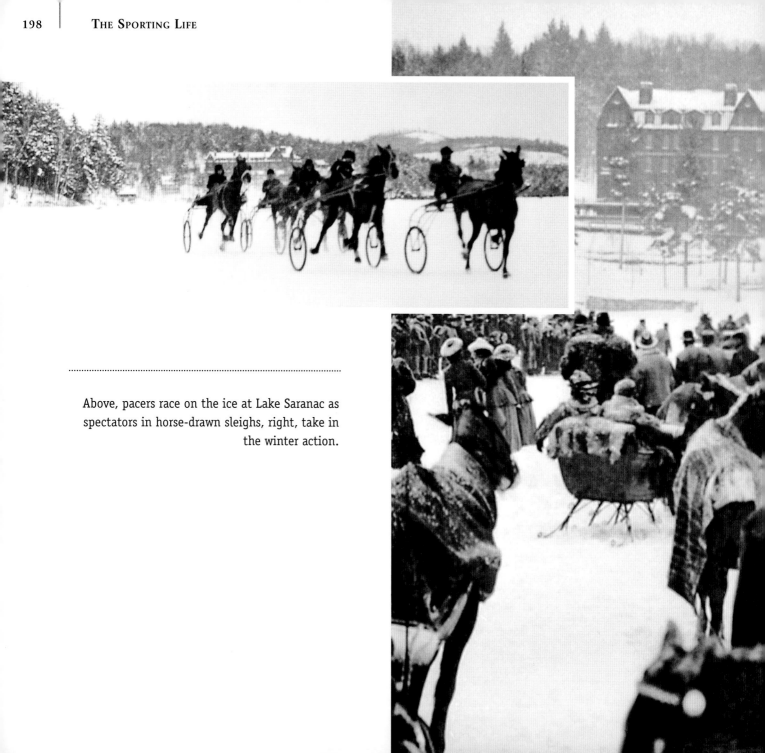

Above, pacers race on the ice at Lake Saranac as spectators in horse-drawn sleighs, right, take in the winter action.

The Meadow Brook Hunt Club is one of the nation's oldest, with foxhunting taking place near Hempstead, Long Island, as early as 1768. The club, enamored of British traditions, early in the twentieth century, took to calling farmers over whose land members rode as the "tenantry," according to the *New York Times*. "Ever since the Meadow Brook Hunt Club instituted the fox-hunting business on Long Island, there has been friction between the society people who ride cross country and the natives, who at that time were known as farmers and who own the land. Generous compensation for broken fences and ruined crops has never effectually closed up the breach," the paper reported.

ACKNOWLEDGMENTS

Eclipse Press wishes to thank Cathy Schenck, head librarian for the Keeneland Association, for her participation in *Best of the Widener Collection*. Schenck helped select photos, wrote the foreword, and reviewed the final product.

The following members of Eclipse Press provided research and caption information: Rena Baer, Jacqueline Duke, and Tom Hall. Graphic artists Beth McCoy and Brian Turner designed the book and imaging specialist David Young edited the photographs.